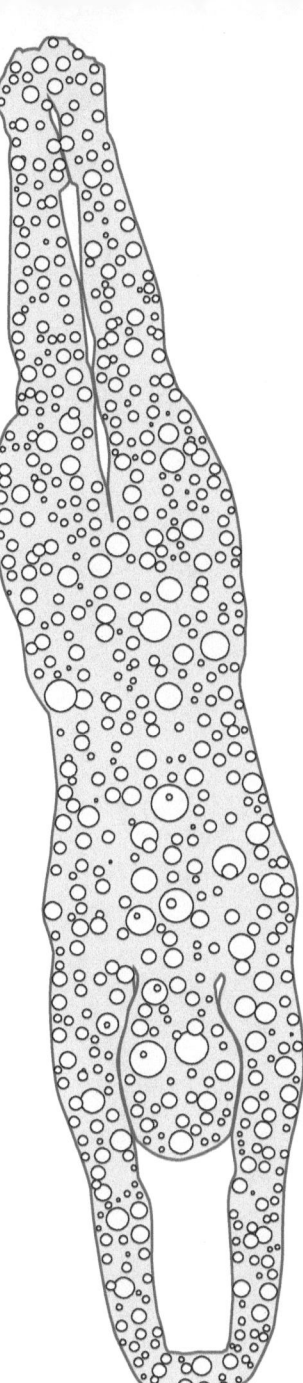

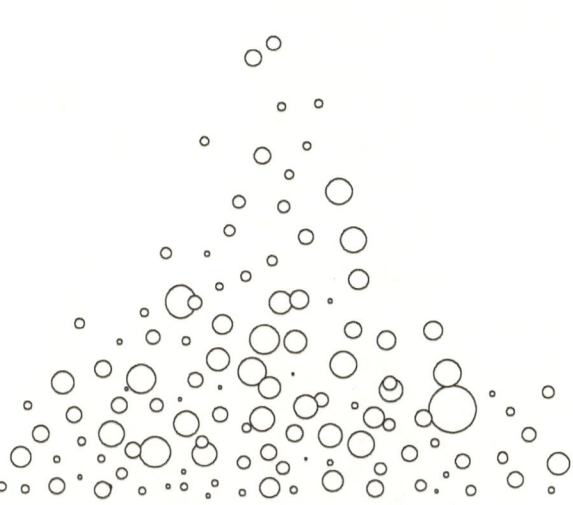

# Pools of June
## Mary Meriam

EXOT BOOKS
NEW YORK

exotbooks.com
First Edition
Copyright 2022 Mary Meriam
All Rights Reserved
Design: Julio M. Perea
Typeset in Baskerville & Orpheus Pro
ISBN: 978-1-7358236-3-8

For Lillian

&

the Backers
the Barbers
the Binders
the Blurbers
the Critters
the Editors
the Farmers
the Friends
the Lesbians
the Mistresses
the Poets
the Prompters
the Publishers
and
the Reviewers
for their
prodding
encouragement
nurturance
and inspiration
for which
I am truly
grateful

# Contents

Carrie's House  1

Trans*  2

Black Bark  3

Laurel's Leaving  5

Roxanne, Witch  6

Serious Doll  7

Eos  8

Needlepoint Point  9

Charm  10

Dear Heart  11

Farewell, Farcia  12

Late Fall  13

Wind  14

The Gray-Green Trouble at the End of the Ant  15

Allegory of the Known and Unknown  16

Ghazal of Going  17

Where I Wait (18)

Mother Tree (19)

Seven Sad Stories (20)

The Bee's Rage (21)

Wish (22)

Dictionary of Owl (24)

This I (25)

The Lost Crown (27)

The Rudiments of Ruby (35)

Tender Pour (39)

Beads (40)

Mysterious Darling (43)

Trees (44)

Handwritten (45)

Fruits (46)

Carol and I were lovers (48)

Transplanted (49)

One Time with Tam (51)

Singer (52)

She Writes to Her (53)

Arrive (56)


Notes (61)

Acknowledgments (63)

About the Author (65)

# Carrie's House

I built a house of driftwood.
I built a house of stone.
I built a house to be alone.
I built a house that stood.

Who called the owl to visit me?
Who whistled for the crow?
Who grew my lovely pecan tree?
What does the robin know?

I told the world the story of
My complicated love.

# Trans*

Drown me now, sailor.
Fir fir fir fir, o little white blossom, save me.

She misses her mother, had a few surgeries.
Now these wings on my back and a mustache.

Now she's telling me her dreams and nightmares.
Just get off my back, this is my map.

Sleepy, erudite, easy, ooooo, bat legs, foxy.
No way will I have a birded head.

Then she starts blooming into a striped wallflower.
No one could look at the brown blind little creature.

Take this red road to Rahway. You will find the sticks.
The sticks will be bats. Toss them into the sea.

# Black Bark

*After Ana Mendieta's "Tree of Life"*

I decided I wanted to be a black girl.
If I couldn't be a black girl
I'd be a white girl but I didn't want to be
a white girl.

I find a tree and drag the bark on my skin,
some grasses and earth, until I am black
by the sweat of my own skin.

I'm caught by a pool and captured and shipped
someplace else.
It's such a shitty thing they do to me
but it's only the first shitty thing.
One shitty thing after another happens.

I wonder why the goddess I pray to
allows this to happen.
I don't know her anymore,
and no one knows me anymore.

I will not titillate you with sordid confessions,
nor will I dwell upon the horrors inflicted upon me.
Instead, I will eat the black beans of my own skin.

It was a dangerous decision to become a black girl.
I didn't know my skin would be a red flag,
and my people would be lynched.
But I feel better not being white,
since it's the whites in charge that lynch
black girls like me
whether they knot the rope or not.

Whether or not you know it or not,
the tree where they tie the rope
is the tree that bathes my black skin
with tree mercy and consolation
so my black soul wiggles loose from the noose,
junks its losses, and slips past them.

# Laurel's Leaving

She alone moon-howls trees' leaves down,
fashions a strapless fall gown,

garlands bare skin with snake-greens
culled from neighborhood queens,

a hat plucked from holly and fir,
then lets those heels that crippled her

die at the moss-rich trunk base
coated with white mildew lace,

and steps barefoot to the scene
on holy ground arrow-clean.

She alone leaves sadness for
a most curious shutting of the door,

a social life in a different town,
a myth, a switcheroo, a buckle-down.

Now she is a tree unshod, unzipped,
she carries greenery fresh and clipped

under a moon undergoing eclipse,
a whole-hearted she with a she she strips.

# Roxanne, Witch

They said I could be a witch if
I lifted a strand of my hair without touching it
on a windless day in a meadow
when clouds make black and white shadows.

My hair grows fast in tangled curls
longer than my teeth and twice as surly.
My name is Roxanne LaBaptista Lorraine.
Stare at me and I'll stare you down the dirty drain.

Tell me to smile, I'll use my hair as a weapon
to strangle you, who think you have power.
For I have the strength of rage on my side
and delicate tendrils adorning my eyes.

My beauty is a yellow bird in a cedar forest,
nesting there, flying on broomsticks for food.
The music I bear on my burdened back
is mine, brother, so remember your lack.

# Serious Doll

Her hand is reaching into space for you.
She tries to organize her face for you.

No man can touch her plastic hollowness.
Her big uplifted eyes say grace for you.

See drops of water roll across her cheeks.
She cannot find a breathing place for you.

The current runs away in strange directions.
In fields she gathers Queen Anne's lace for you.

Hasn't she heard you speaking to the sea?
She puts the flowers in this vase for you.

Measure that never stops, unending stairs,
the unknown finish in the race for you.

Her secret cabinet is locked away.
May mercy win the jeweled case for you.

# Eos

Hopeless, asking hells in the sky, the storming
mud-pie slinger, hacking the weak to pieces,
dawn of bitter sickening habit-forming
fucked-up deforming.

My own Eos, covering turf with morning
dewdrops, make my coverage and headlines charming,
make my local personal times non-harming,
nothing alarming.

May your softness often restore, bring warming
speeches, peaches, fields full of tiger lilies,
larks, and not too terribly hard, your calming
cloak, so disarming.

# Needlepoint Point

Sick gauze from sutures in the sky, o bump, o thump, o thing
Gallop dearful thready, you in the haystack threshing
Weren't we there once, weren't we at a canter field-wise
Egg lump shells neat in rows in the hen house hiding
Cats at the rodent doors neatly chew, chew, chomp
We darn each other till cows pick the path home
And I am I circulating blood and air and wanting
And you are every lovely leaping doe and lonely tale

# Charm

My rooster sleeps the sleepe of birds
free to fly the drifting sky.

My hen divides hir eggs in thirds
and warms thim with hir loving eye.

My peaceful flower beds begin
releasing spring and blossoming.

My roof keeps cozy feelings in
while winter haz hir final fling.

My windows tell the world to staye
a distance from my silver sink.

My door will make ye go awaye
or knocks or bells will make it blink.

Repeat these stanzas like a spell
till ye are well, and all is well.

# Dear Heart

All the times I misunderstood, forgive me.
I could go downhill in a sled with sorrow.
Snow, my hero, build me a fort this winter
made of your hollow

hub of pulsing chambers, your crimson center.
Greenless branches stick me like Venus arrows.
Why, my Valentine, did she leave me stricken,
frozen, and slighted?

Once, she slid her fingers inside my velvet
cushion, knit my cap, and embroidered borders,
dressed me all the way to the silver heavens.
Oh, she was lovely

who could heal a storm through the tangled briars,
who could soothe a flood through the scalding trials,
who could kiss an oath through the fallen oak trees,
terrace the traumas.

# Farewell, Farcia

Don't try my patience, gentle telephone.
Go split your wires, crack your hand-set bone,
go digital, go slow, go beat a drum,
go ring yourself to death. I will not come.

I'll hear instead the doves cry overhead.
So still I'll stay, she'll surely think I'm dead
to love; but no, I hear the loving doves
that fit together like two hands in gloves.

The doves fly west to east and east to west.
But why? Because doves know love has no rest.
The doves compose me with their loving song
transforming into goodness what is wrong.

And I remain below, a single one
like every other single in the sun,
taking a walk in the dim dove-land wood.
Farewell, Farcia, farce will bring no good.

# Late Fall

I sit outside without my e-devices,
a maniac in freezing breezes, ink
almost unflowing, fingers chilled, my crises
on hold but planning mutinies of stink.
I rise and raise my sword to strike them down.
One vain and petty Temporal Thief strikes first
but I throw books at it and make it drown.
Inside the icy lake, its pockets burst.
The Prince of Patience fills my bank account
with merry jests. The Queen of Questions drops
her ring beside my plate. Sad Knight will mount
my stairs and shake her hair until it stops
shaking all over me, a kind of warfare.
At that point, I discard my sword somewhere.

# Wind

From spring to summer is a slow striptease.
Gone first, the hat, the socks, the heavy pants
for lighter pants, bare arms, and soon, romance
of skin and air, the touches of a breeze
who cries to me, *I am your spirit lover.*
*I know you, you are mine invisibly.*
*I move the heavens for your company,*
*we two unbound in love with one another.*
A thousand new green leaves begin to wave
and whisper near the water where I live.
Wind sighs that she has everything to give
in spring, and tries with all her scent to save
my flowers. *Feel me better, lonely girl.*
*Unwrap your limbs the more the more I twirl.*

# The Gray-Green Trouble at the End of the Ant

She catnaps beside me, my little companion,
soft spring steams light streaming over us
from the billowing sunless sky of soft gray clouds
soft as her gray fur, soft as fresh bird calls,
soft as the hundred shades of green I see
in this forest home, our foot on earth.
We breathe gently listening to the lapping lake
and trouble boards a boat and drifts away.
Still, some sadness sticks around, some woe,
some loss I can't get over renewing itself
like ants in spring crawling the counters.
I put out borax traps, they throng them
thinking the bait is sweet that later kills them.
I can never forget my spring is bittersweet.

# Allegory of the Known and Unknown

Down the driveway, a Deer in the woods, and we look at each other,
sunlit nose black and wet. Crows peck a bloody Opossum on the road.
I am to leave without breakfast, return near noon for Minestrone.
At the supermarket, Michael signs to me about a trip to Florida,
soon, soon. He teaches me to sign "wow, great." Michael smiles
and signs and speaks all at once. Michael carries my bags.
Michael teaches me to sign "take care" and "hello" and "goodbye."
Driving to town, clusters of Naked Ladies. At the little market,
a big bouquet of Naked Ladies. Patty invites me to her party,
to walk through her field of Naked Ladies. Christine the Oblivious
Checkout Clerk rings me up for one Parsley bunch but there are
two bunches in the bag. At the moment, Christine forgets
the name for tomatoes. She wears sparkling gauzy blue scarves,
clothing art. The Potatoes, the Celery. At the Farmers Market,
Andrew has Carrots, his wife Madeleine almost due, he says,
in a snow storm. Driving a narrow road on a steep wooded hill,
the window open it's so warm, a Fox appears to my left,
about ten feet From Me, on a clear hill Above Me, a beautiful color
and shape, alert, graceful, lovely. I stop and stare, the Fox stares
back At Me, into my eyes!! I skip the Post Office, what could be there.
On the road home, a feeling Strikes Me of utter aloneness.
How is this possible. I drag in the bags, work again
at the screen for hours, in the kitchen again work for hours.
I want to see you. You have come to my home in the mountains,
you have come to my home by the sea, you have come to my home
in a clean city of enlightened citizens with advanced degrees
and organic gardens. I've been reading *Odd Girl Out* on the couch.
You've been taking a taxi from the airport. Dusk soothes the space
under the vaulted ceilings of my living room. A fragrant breeze
from the terrace stirs the shades with a slight sigh. "There you are."

# Ghazal of Going

She rises like a secret meant for me alone
and tilts the shattered glass of light at sea alone.

Where light on waves lays a mosaic and a moan,
serious birds descend unhappily alone.

Repeat the secret monthly, kiss her collarbone,
and when she travels blindly, let her be alone.

The lifelong lonely ones still listening for the phone
will live alone on mountains silently alone.

How pleasing the tiny point in time of being known,
sun on the golden leaves of one lit tree alone.

She weakens through unpeopled dreams at night, the groan
of old pianos sounding middle C alone.

Look in the kitchen where she's grinding stone on stone
to see the habitat of bee Marie alone.

# Where I Wait

I wait in honeysuckle thunder,
the sharp alarming cries of crows.
A storm approaching never blows
my long undone undoing under.
I hear sweet distant mourning doves,
nearby woodpecker's rhythmic tap.
Suddenly leaves stand still in sap,
hot sun, and sound. I wait for Love's
hand on my shoulder, "Hey lost one,
stuck-in-the-woods, you bird-girl-leaf
who sings in springs without belief,
don't trash your dope. I am not done."
At that, the breeze returns and lifts
a forest-full of greeny gifts.

# Mother Tree

Knot-knowing tree in all her innocence
stands in her stand (for standing is her way),
mingling her roots with roots, her leaves so dense
in canopy, they almost block the day.
Inside this tree's green palm, a girl at play
swings on her swing, her bare legs light in air,
the motion soothing her and her dismay,
the kindest time her life has known, and rare.
The tree inside her mind is like a prayer
that says this moment will forever be
remembered. Now the sun sets in a flare,
and sunlight floods her chapel of the tree.
Her swinging stops, the fields' long shadows grow,
she leaves the leaves who may or may not know.

# Seven Sad Stories

Once my hand in the rain, my foot in rivers
Twice my eyes and my shoulders told my story
Knelt with nothing to pray in crowded shelters
Lost my papers in mudslides slid down sideways
Found my child but her arms were slit with sugar
Fired shot from a failure looks like killing
Any sweet goes to yellow rust and tumor

# The Bee's Rage

I would find things I could use,
even things not for children my age.
It was how I said the things I meant.
It's where my pigeon years were spent
mucking about in the backyard ooze,
making mud casseroles with a tin toy stove,
where I retreated to boil the bee's rage.
This ivy leaf, what a garnish it will make.
Let me glue it closed with pigeon spittle.
Here's a faucet by the chimney bricks.
Here are blades of grass and bite-size sticks,
every pretty stone just the right kind of little.
How much frost, how much flare will it take
to turn my sickly pigeon into dove.

# Wish

Watch it out
breathy lift
and roll around
the grass the cat
would like
wood love
the fallen leaves
the bugs
to catch a squirrel
to bite its neck
alarm the blood
vampire eyes
then the cow sound
get a hamburger
for fake breakfast
get a egg cracked
so you say your hunger
lasts your life long
it couldn't last long
it couldn't it couldn't
it isn't their name
it would release from it
look off dreaming
come back player
needle in groove
childhood room
bite that rat's neck
cat's hunger wish
bite that worm
bird's fly wish
who could kill a cow?
those big brown peepers

holding a soul
*on a wagon bound for market*
so she sang the death
and made life from it
and sadness so we weep
never having a choice
this is your blood wish
not mine
a bean-eater
a lopsided lorry
carries carrion
marbled blood
ice-packed flesh
no sweat stuck in fur
grooming unknown
a gentle hand
a solemn vow
a broken cycle
bird's wing broke
in the dead leaves
more wonder
that cat would find
and yet a fox
might bite her neck
so she stays inside
a captive cat
scratching boxes
posing in shadows
in a race she wins
by living

# Dictionary of Owl

Who cares about the redbud tree, its flowers
half-black, half-pink, from winter's April freeze;
who cares who lives halfway or dies too soon,
the blue jay's baby squirming on bare ground,
the agonies of blood, the frigid breeze
shaking the fragile sense of April showers;
who cares who craves the heated pools of June,
the lake of boaters buzzing by or drowned.
Two vultures meet me at my open door,
scanning for carrion, the stink of spasms,
the sky-gods pecking rotting flesh for food;
who cares if this strange order ends in good,
or if the chickadee lands in the chasms
of endless carelessness forevermore.

# This I

This is a monument to I.
This speaks for I
and for more than I;
this speaks for the culture. In every culture, parts of I
are suppressed, restricted, criminalized. Rarely, true I
are forged in restrictive cultures. Often, restrictions suffocate, and the I's
creativity (if not the actual I)
is crushed. But the I
who survives and grows can create a monument to I.

I
forged by restriction form a subculture of survival. In gulags, Russian I,
in death camps, Jewish I,
Black I,
Women I,
Gay and Lesbian I,
all face cultures that suppress I,
restrict, punish, torture, murder I.

Charlotte Mew burned most of this, then killed her I.
To survive, an I
might hide or disguise I,
as Gertrude Stein did by writing in I,
as Amy Lowell did by avoiding I.

This serves as a substitute culture where the towns and cities of I
are honored. If the I
is denied pen and paper, then I
serves as pen and paper. If I
in a nursing home can grow a flower of I
by writing this, then she is blooming, and for a moment, I.
If I

in a death camp can hold on to the scrap of paper in his pocket that
 holds this, he is I.

Paul Celan wrote, "Only one thing remained reachable, close and
 secure amid all losses: this I."


While the I
works to save this, this also works to save the I.
The I
is heroic who can survive restrictions and build a monument to I.

Langston Hughes wrote, "no great I has ever been afraid of being I."

If I
wish to be considered, I
should remember the difference between ordinary I-
suffering and the suffering caused by the culture's restriction of I.

# The Lost Crown

1.
I stop to gaze for minutes at the moon
that gazes back at me from outer space,
touches the outer limits of my face,
light touch. I'm lost just like the fat raccoon
descending frontwards down the dying oak
in afternoon, the bandit full of rats
that race lakeside at night like diplomats
of war. I could remember how she spoke,
how many minutes in the years I've lost,
how tall the spangly trees below the sky,
but it would only make my moon-face cry.
How little does it boot how hard I'm tossed
by my full moon and moon of my quagmire
that rises like those horses fleeing fire.

2.
I watch those helpless horses fleeing fire
in a video of California burning.
A group of six or so are trotting, turning
from tree to burning tree as if the dire
inferno is a muddled game of chance.
They acted calm, but weren't they terrified?
There was no place to flee the underside,
going as one, to death, they trot, they dance.
Fairies can't breathe the dirty smoke, my dear.
What will we do without a breath of air?
I try to find a fairy here and there,
someone to last a life with no one near.
Impossibly, I spot how you inspire,
ponder the deepening blue of my desire.

3.
I ponder blue, the depth of my desire,
my blue of tears, my blue of sighs, my blue
that sees you smiling at a distance, you
my work of art, my soothing, shocking choir.
You hold the note so long, I lose my grip
so let me bring you here this time in verse.
Couldn't the circumstances be much worse?
Here sits a body, reined and sturdy, whip
discarded for a stricter inner boss,
sits by the old and ugly oak the owl
once slept in. In my mind, coyote-howl
and now the day begins to end, across
the lake three geese fly low. I hear their tune,
wonder if birds still call this late, this soon.

4.
If any bird still calls this late, this soon,
I answer, calling too, too, too, for this
remembrance of the air in bird-call bliss.
I'm tangled up in Time just like the loon
that makes a V-mark in the mirror-lake
moving the waves and clouds to suit its trail.
I failed to save my sister. I still fail.
This day, this night, this life, this endless ache.
I saved myself, and that was hard enough,
(dear sister, may I speak to you this way
and tell you all the things I need to say?)
I see the beast that ravaged you, how tough
its hide, how hot its fangs, how slick its slime,
and then I take a trip through icy Time.

5.
And then I take a trip through icy Time
but icy why? No sisters on the quest
to answer, once again I fail the test
to be in sync with history's sublime,
you know, those moments of coincidence
when who you are is like a raucous crow
slicing the air in sections, each a foe
felled, and your I goes free, flies the fence.
You bring a bag of roasted nuts and seeds,
some ripening bananas, and some water,
wearily plod the earth, a raging daughter,
die and return to gardens full of weeds
that need hot touches of the marigold,
circle the planets' nipples, statue-cold.


6.
Circle the planets' nipples, statue-cold,
not knowing where to land your little ship,
on rocky cliffs or islands, or the tip
of continents, or in the ocean's old
and endless rocking cradle. You must go,
carry your cases loaded up with weight,
and shed as best you can the armor plate
trying to crush your tendrils so, and so,
and so I trek from hell to tell my story,
a girl Odysseus inside, a "sir"
to strangers in my hat of phony fur,
defying every polar category.
Then like Penelope, I dart and fold,
chant the enchantment I was never told.

7.
Chant the enchantment I was never told
on school and sick days, weekends, holidays,
enchantment fled like minutes in a haze
of suffocating fog that rose and rolled.
Impossible to go too far, you cry,
but you learned early how to laugh. You laugh
and throw your mittens in the air, a gaffe
you're sorry for, and yet you don't know why,
why mittens, why not gloves, why winter bells
not summer songs, why river not the ocean,
why does his singing spark this strong emotion
when clearly you are subject to her spells?
You check your clock in Central Standard Time,
count the believers lost with every chime.

8.
Count the believers lost with every chime
and if the sky is gray and overcast,
count the unraked and withered leaves that last
all winter, building fertile beds of grime.
I give you these instructions hopefully
and couched in prayer, my hands held still and strong
with palm to palm, to cleanse the world of wrong,
of mockery and harm of life, so lowly.
Then the horizon glows in pastel pinks,
the wind acknowledges my thoughts, and skims
like icicles through darkened twigs and limbs.
The forest skirts grow deeper red, ice rinks
of clouds begin to turn a dusky blue.
Now they are stars in orbit burning through.

9.
Now they are stars in orbit burning through
a skyful of believers, holes of hope
and wishful dreaming. I'm the kind of dope
whose blood gets squeezed by things I cannot do.
You sit imagining. You run to help.
Your running shoes are broken down and shot
but you don't notice. You are simply not
secure or calm enough to save yourself.
You sit and make pathetic xmas cards
and send them out to strangers who don't care,
a prisoner without a breath of air
whose food is stolen by the prison guards.
I call myself on memory's telephone,
my flesh, my eyes. My breath creates its own.

10.
My flesh, my eyes, my breath creates its own
body of flash, lies, death, a mallard duck
of love who hasn't found a lake of luck.
The duck is young, perhaps, but seems alone,
flapping its wings too hard to reach the tree,
then little peep peep peep peeps, and I
can only listen since I mustn't fly.
You didn't understand your starving sea.
Forgive yourself for that and try again.
Crow on the sidewalk. Chase the girl to bed.
Take these directions with you in your head.
You called a number not in service then.
But now it rings in heaven freshly blown
rhythms, composes its discordant tone.

11.
Rhythm composes the discordant tone
of heartbeats beaten down. O minus one,
will bitchy talk to me? Estrangement won
for salty years the mother's mucky throne.
The sun illuminates an eagle in
the window and a ring of mooching crows,
a show of ruling power ratios
bird-balancing on branches, one kingpin.
Look how its yellow beak stabs at the fish
it caught. Its giant claws afflict the flesh.
Its golden wings a net of fishing mesh.
Perhaps the eagle had a latent wish,
only a moment's peace before it flew,
willing the caws to stop for just a few.

12.
Willing the caws to stop for just a few
flutters of peace, but nothing liberates.
The pack of dogs surrounds you like the fates
you fled, and there is nothing you can do
except survive, and try again, and hold
my hand. I'm reaching now for every sister hurt,
flung and discarded, scrounging in the dirt,
who needs the solace of her story told.
Their spirits speak to me in rustling trees,
the soft and changing clouds, the stars at night,
the Seven Sisters multiplied, that call the light
earthward to open doors with magic keys.
Repeat my humble prayer in beating heart
seconds, to let the clocks of quiet start.

13.
Seconds before the clocks of quiet start,
bodies of water still. Your body craves
the sleep and fall and dream of subtle waves,
the nighttime's sweet unfathomable part.
The lonely patterns of the lake, the lost
forever from this world, the panther found
still living in the wilderness, the sound
that wakes you wide-eyed, how this losing cost
much more than you could ever hope to make.
You may not ever fall asleep again.
You mark your bearings with a fountain pen.
The fountain overflows, becomes the lake.
You dedicate yourself to making art.
Why does Time keep tearing us apart?

14.
Why does Time keep tearing us apart?
You ask as if the ending isn't sad,
as if Time's charity was what you had,
and afterwards, Time's tatters will depart.
But you're invisible; Time won't reply.
Listen to how the rain begins to stop
then beats your roof again, each water drop
another tear that trembles in your eye.
You search the cloudy sky for answers to
questions of Time. The rain resolves to fall
again, on nights that knock against your wall
like ghosts without a home, without a boo.
When bright winds blow the midnight past the noon,
I stop to gaze for minutes at the moon.

15.
I stop to gaze for minutes at the moon
that rises like those horses fleeing fire,
ponder the deepening blue of my desire,
wonder if birds still call this late, this soon.
And then I take a trip through icy Time,
circle the planets' nipples, statue-cold,
chant the enchantment I was never told,
count the believers lost with every chime.
Now they are stars in orbit burning through
my flesh, my eyes. My breath creates its own
rhythm, composes its discordant tone,
willing the caws to stop for just a few
seconds, to let the clocks of quiet start.
Why does Time keep tearing us apart?

# The Rudiments of Ruby

I, the witch that walks the earth
I, the witch that bathes in water

I, the witch of work of worth
I, the witch that walks the earth

I, the witch attending my birth
I, the witch and desperate daughter

I, the witch that walks the earth
I, the witch that bathes in water

Chartreuse Aura
Orb of Consequence

My abode of preference and address
Where I may amble with pride

Coincides with a quarry of fire ants
A sense of place is so very important

Oh so deadly and helpful, so you see
I could not have been at the crime scene

Come forth, as I like to say to the elders
My circle is the third turn in Vineyville

I am a Witch of the Fourth Square

I live at leaves tree-side
My eyelids like the lake

Gaze at evening's slide
To deeper greener leaves

Drift if you wish with me
The slightest breezes lift

The curtain of the heat
I see you rippling into bliss

This is my window into you
Raucous thrilling nights

Sleep and dreams dimmed
The darkness flies

Drawing feathered tree buds lightly
Falling and filling a wonder trunk of lives

The pink of cloudy dots paints evening brightly
No kidding how the hawk, a black dash, dives

To catch a creature from the forest floor
November, trilling still, glows golden gray

We could have been
The flames of forgetfulness

A history written somewhere uncertain
Those jars buried beneath the dead

Little children dead from neglect
Torn between evil and good

Sheets of paper to start a fire
Or flowers

Thursday evening, rainfall trickling
I have dinner, seeds and fresh apples after

On the lake a shadow alights, an ancient
Absence of knowledge

Scholars wonder who was her favorite lover
Lovely, ugly, women, or men, they quarrel

Phantom, mortal, suicide, teacher, goddess

Fool behind the moon and a mask of weather
Quick as lightning flashes across the treeline

Interstellar shock like the visions chanced on
Moment swinging tight like a trip to Venus

Saved in my hindsight
Held for the future

In my desert, you are rain
Replenishing wells in my hills

You teach me pool tongue
I had never spoken it before with a woman

My thirst wakes me and stays the night
You are the cool cup on the shelf

Is this moment one drop of water
Lost like the flowers between us?

Let me drink you
My earth cracks and waits

I have the schedule for the ferry
Wave to me soon

# Tender Pour

It keeps pouring    how the green rain
Oh don't say    love    rain    green
Her vigilance    her lightning    her absence
Oh don't say again    how the green rain
Pours on oak that drinks it
It's in mountains    not in city
It cracks near me    I'm not afraid
Should I be    yes    I should be scared
It could hit the oak    (or me)    the weighted
Blue orange light    the thunder louder rain
Harder rain    louder thunder    on the oak
Too dark to see between the leaves
Humidity ushers in fall    sharp soaks
This stand I call my yard    tall trees
Lake rising to it    rain falling in it
Tiny mist drops on my naked arms
My cozy chair    who is subject to this rain
And helpless in it

# Beads

I open
my blue-
berries

and when
the wind
I speak of

so often
from the lake
laps my lap

a jumble of
fake
pearls

smooths itself
to strands
pinned

lavishly
on my
neck.

It's how
I think of you,
and how

your berries
please me
nights

when all my
eyes
are closed

and lights
fade
into fairy

tulips
but you
stay true.

If she
hadn't stung
my face,

if rain
would
soak

the
terrible
ground,

if a
single
bee

made the
loudest
sound,

perhaps I'd
keep
my necklace

in a case,
hidden
from every

view
except
your eyes

that see
me thru
my cries.

# Mysterious Darling

Quiet. The squirrel hugs a limb.
The cat curls round her dreams of prey.
Only the leaves newborn in May
whisper with birdsongs on the rim
of sound. I whisper in her ear
*I love you so*. Then stand away,
glad to have finally had my say,
warm with the blush of her this near.
Crashing. The noisy world returns,
insisting that I am not hers,
and drowns my band of whisperers.
So through the years, my spirit learns
that once in spring, a lover's dream
is truer than the truth might seem.

## Trees

I love this screen of oak and maple trees
hiding me from the boaters on the lake.
I love the fattened leaves in summer's breeze

singing the forest full of symphonies.
When I have any love-life left to make,
I love this screen of oak and maple trees.

When burdened by my sad, old memories,
the screeching hawk, the tick, the lying snake,
I love the fattened leaves in summer's breeze,

their veiny palms and festive shapes, the bees
and hummingbirds that sip them as they shake.
I love this screen of oak and maple trees

the way most people love their families.
For having none, and for my longing's sake,
I love the fattened leaves in summer's breeze.

I listen to the play of green degrees
of pitch and key, the greens the breezes wake
forming this screen of oak and maple trees
bearing the fattened leaves in summer's breeze.

# Handwritten

How drunk with longing one can be for hands,
for her hot love, her knowing me, her hands.

Cicadas buzz and hum in forest trees.
Relentlessly the summer sweats my hands.

They say she stayed away from human touch,
a spirit pure as sky. Then we hold hands.

The insects, birds, and bark, the leaves in air,
the leaving day, the memory of hands.

How wild the dirt, how soon the soaking storm.
In my green canopy, the clock-face hands.

The peace of lapping waves, the sobs of herons,
the place in heaven I may see her hands.

# Fruits

I don't suppose she's read Wu Tsao.
She must be half my age, and yet, with those
fine Chinese eyes, she climbs inside
my eyes as if she knows me, confident
that I, at least, accept her rainbow pride
and dykey style. I do, young one, as
kneeling to bag my apples from a lower bin,
I feel her sink her city gaze into
my tank-top's low-cut top.

heavy hay, soaked dirt
dig potatoes then
catch ride back to town

cut-glass disco beat
strobe-lit
blue-jeaned balls

torch on her tank top
naked muscles,
green eyes

trembling cherry, kiwi,
blushing mango
shake it all down

October sky
distant Andromeda
clean sheets on our cold bed

la lune almost full
gauzy clouds
in my window

Angus head
half-cow, half-bear
black as your lover's hair

black cows in the night
awake by the creek
mist rolling in the valley

# Carol and I were lovers

Then Carol introduced me to Elizabeth
Bishop, her handshake cool and tiny, not like Carol's.

Unlike my lover's hot and eager hands, at least
Briefly, until Camille distracted me from Carol.

A few years later, Carol met me at the Y's
Ashbery reading. I was at Columbia.

Carol had flown from San Francisco with her money.
Oh she was rich, and free to visit NYC.

She took me to her lavish suite. The doorman seemed
Upset by me. Perhaps he smelled my rented room.

I can't recall the reading. Lush and packed, no doubt.
Carol and I on 92nd, her arm up.

The taxi stops for us, but who jumps in but John,
Stealing our taxi like he owns the street, not sorry.

We're two invisibles as lesbians, young poets,
Excluded in 1980. Ash in our eyes.

# Transplanted

"You seem to know your way around the city,"
she says, turning from the piano
and the tiny statuettes of geniuses.
I send her a letter.
Flight patterns branch out
forests of airports
the letter is distant as the diamond window
on a ship to Venus.
The day the idiots converge
on the Hudson barges, with flags, cheers,
and souvenirs, I receive her reply:
*pleasure in other directions.*

At the entrance to the park
thick stench of dogshit
piles of cut gray branches
and a view of patches of dirt
where games kill the grass.
I sit on a bench reading
in a haze of cherry petals.
"Why aren't we lovers?"
she says in your dream
the strange girl you tried to love
who steals your sleep
in a drugged sprawl.

"She does that all the time,"
the drinkers at The Duchess say
blood in the bathroom sink
from the girl who slits her wrists.
Frantic, I race
up and down the staircase.

It's 1981, I think,
the same damn lovesick
song on the jukebox
the slower suicide dykes, rooted to the bar
and my pale wild hunger
as I carry rum and cokes to every dancer.

The heart-shaped mole on your cheek
says love me. Your eyes embrace me.
We strip. Your hands and your mouth
travel my body as mine travel yours.
No black night possible, just the color
of rose, dying on the air
four weak stars in the park
the dark-eyed fuchsia dying
in the heavily gated window
rattled by trains.
I want the roar and rustle
of dark expanse, crazy leaves, solitude.

I sit on the fire escape while day grows dusky
scanning the streets for the taxi she drives.
Eclipse night,
we circle Manhattan island
until she takes me over the bridge to her garden
just beginning to bear ripe red tomatoes.
Catbirds sing and ruffle their feathers
attracted to pale trumpet vines
in the suburb dawn.
Surrounded by scents,
I want to lie down
and flower.

# One Time with Tam

In SoHo while the wealthy dined,
we talked, we walked, along the street
to your stop. My stop. We don't mind

that we don't stop, nor go to find
the dark below, the empty seat.
In SoHo while the wealthy dined,

we spent a while, and you were kind,
your murmurs on the sidewalk sweet.
Your stop. My stop. We don't mind.

Go home, go home, the city whined.
Go take your train. Still on our feet,
in SoHo while the wealthy dined,

you sensed, perhaps, that pit and rind
were all I had at home to eat.
Your stop. My stop. We don't mind,

so closely have our steps aligned,
and you were all I had of heat,
in SoHo while the wealthy dined.
Your stop. My stop. We don't mind.

# Singer

Just when I think I can talk to her, I lose my voice.
My fat tongue stuck and lips too shy confuse my voice.

I drag my vocal chords through awkward exercises,
race up and down the hills, like this unscrews my voice.

But still can't talk to her. I have too much to say
or feel too much. My springing spirit slews my voice.

She takes me to her friend's apartment, maybe lover.
She talks, she says. She does. It seems to bruise my voice.

It seems like she has verbal lovers everywhere.
She introduces us. If I could use my voice.

She loves me singing in her choir, and I sing
her music perfectly in tune. She woos my voice.

All this was years ago, in crushing times, and yet
my customary solitude still skews my voice.

# She Writes to Her

Elaine once stood in music's breeze,
conducting me in choirs and kisses,
in Bach's *Christ lag in Todesbanden*,
the alto mating the soprano
in a duet that etched a lesbian nation
in my chest. It was the seventies.
I stood alone in death's dark closet,
silence surrounding my secret glaring
strangeness until the day I met
Elaine, my only breeze and breath.
For her, I sang in every language
standing in her stand of trees,
suddenly in tune, open as heaven,
released from underground, and safe
in her leaves. She taught with hands
and scores the music I needed to start
my pen in motion, a little binder
of love lyrics I wrote to her.
Elaine illuminated me.
I stood alone in the dark auditorium
adoring her light, watching her play
first cello in the symphony rehearsal.
From the banks of a small stream in summer
she watched me naked in a waterfall,
and we danced all night in disco sparkles.
Then she left me, left me alone.
But she left me with a loving note.

Sometimes the light of dusk or morning
takes me to Sophie's healing, the pale
or powerful colors where we loved,
fields we walked in, hills we climbed,

roads we traveled, planes we took
to and from Tortola, the sea
we swam, the beds we made lesbian.
She drew me forth and took my picture.
I tilled her garden and mixed her paint.
We showed our poems to each other.
Do you understand the wealth
of color, my deer? Of line, my owl?
Each kiss between us another
treasure that fed the poems I wrote
for college, skewing Sophie-love
to silence. How drifty it was to censor.
How fully she filled my arms with gifts
of body and water, how dearly she
was into me, showing me art
exhibited in fancy places
and in her splattered studios,
her true paintings blinded by dealers.
So we held half-in, half-out,
dangling and dancing and losing our minds,
the bodies of fish in a clear creek
surrounded by vivid mountains of fate
that tore me in two and left me leaving.

Emily wrote poems to Susie—Wild
nights! Three decades later I learned
what Lillian wrote in the seventies. By then
I'd flooded and drowned three decades, saving
the one marble left of myself. But then
Lillian came billowing down my path
bearing her books, giving her flowers
to me to keep. The whole world bloomed
as I wandered in the land of Lillian—
seeing her writing poems to her—and she
wrote poems to her—and look at her words

to her—and here are more poems of hers
she wrote to her. All this had been hidden,
mocked, erased, buried, burned,
in gardens that could never grow
until unearthed and loved by Lillian.
She gives sunlight and rain and seasons
and makes the earth a welcoming place.
She plucks and prunes, squeezes and clips,
with a touch as light as fairy dust,
until the mysterious scent of sadness
becomes a field of waving daffodils.
I write to her, she writes to me.
I dedicate my books to Lillian
and send them to her distant house
with longing from my leafy trees
and brightness from my flowing pen.

# Arrive

I move hoping you will arrive
while the day and season
are fresh and air
gushes through the window.
I long for your blondness
and young, sleek, white silence.
It is not enough
my veins are stretching
to their limits, snow marks
the upper mountains.

Today, early summer, the honey locusts
snow on the grass and I think
it is snow. I do not wish for
any other season. Hot air stirs me.
You say it is a beautiful night
and ask me to go swimming while
I begin the voice that transforms
as it goes on. To be most concise
is impossible. Like an Italian woman,
I spread over the chair out of my clothes.
Each day is a treasure. Day lilies
sparkle on the dark roadside, an oak
with large and fragrant leaves
leans out of the forest.
You are almost here I imagine
and you are joyful and giving.

Your pale body in the garden makes me weep
as does everything. Is it beauty,
the pure water, my lips that finally fill out
and sing? You bring water to me
in every form. I cry for days,
a horse you ride with broken reins.
The skies are milky, the stars
and your eyes, obscure. Out of summer
and what we have, a hoe, a hammock,
mossy woods, and marshes of lilies,
what will we be able to save?
Will memory be the green earth?

# Notes

"Carrie's House." For Carrie Marry.

"Trans*." https://www.itspronouncedmetrosexual.com/2012/05/what-does-the-asterisk-in-trans-stand-for/

"Farewell, Farcia." Bouts-rimés of Auden's "Funeral Blues."

"Wish." "on a wagon bound for market" is a line from the song "Donna, Donna" recorded by Joan Baez in 1960. The song was originally in Yiddish and called "Dana, Dana."

"This I." Actual quote from Paul Celan: "Only one thing remained reachable, close and secure amid all losses: language. Yes, language. In spite of everything, it remained secure against loss." Actual quote from Langston Hughes: "No great poet has ever been afraid of being himself."

# Acknowledgments

Many thanks to the editors of the following publications, in which these poems appeared, sometimes in earlier versions:

# Journals

*Entropy:* "Tender Pour"
*Lily Poetry Review:* "One Time with Tam"
*Lodestar Quarterly:* "Transplanted"
*Measure:* "Ghazal of Going"
*Poetry:* "Dictionary of Owl"
*Prelude:* "Charm"
*South Florida Poetry Journal:* "Mother Tree"
*Street Spirit:* "This I"
*Subtropics:* "Eos"
*The Ekphrastic Review:* "Trans*", "Black Bark"
*The Gay & Lesbian Review:* "Singer," "Carol and I were lovers"
*The North American Review:* "Needlepoint Point"
*The Raintown Review:* "Wish"
*Wicked Alice:* "Farewell, Farcia"

# Anthologies

*Love Affairs at the Villa Nelle* (Kelsay Books, 2018): "Trees"
*Stonewall Fifty* (Sibling Rivalry Press & Queer Arts Arkansas, 2019): "Arrive"
*Closet Cases: Queers on What We Wear* (Et Alia Press, 2020): "Fruits"

# Chapbook

*The Countess of Flatbroke* (Modern Metrics/Exot Books, 2006): "Farewell, Farcia"

# About the Author

Mary Meriam co-founded Headmistress Press and edits the *Lavender Review: Lesbian Poetry and Art*. She is the author of *My Girl's Green Jacket* (2018) and *The Lillian Trilogy* (2015), both from Headmistress Press. Her other books include *The Countess of Flatbroke* (Modern Metrics/Exot Books, 2006). Poems appear recently in *Poetry, Prelude, Subtropics*, and *The Poetry Review*.

# Other Titles Available From Exot Books

*Huncke*, Rick Mullin ~ 2021
*Schnauzer*, David Yezzi ~ 2018
*Veil On, Veil Off*, John Marcus Powell ~ 2018
*A Special Education*, Meredith Bergmann ~ 2014
*Glorious Babe*, John Marcus Powell ~ 2014
*Questions*, Richard Loranger/Bill Mercer ~ 2013
*Turn*, Ann Drysdale ~ 2013
*Tomorrow & Tomorrow*, David Yezzi ~ 2013
*Facing The Remains*, Tom Merrill ~ 2012
*Blue Wins Forever*, Paco Brown ~ 2012
*They Can Keep The Cinderblock*, Mike Lane ~ 2012
*Colors*, Jay Chollick ~ 2011
*Loony Lovers*, John Marcus Powell ~ 2011
*Filled With Breath: 30 Sonnets by 30 Poets*, ed. Mary Meriam ~ 2010
*Let Me Be Like Glass*, Adriana Scopino ~ 2010
*What's That Supposed To Mean*, Wendy Videlock ~ 2010
*We Internet In Different Voices*, Mike Alexander ~ 2009
*11 Films*, Jane Ormerod ~ 2008
*Aquinas Flinched*, Rick Mullin ~ 2008
*Graceways*, Austin MacRae ~ 2008
*Prospero At Breakfast*, Alan Wickes ~ 2008
*Sometime Before The Bell*, Ray Pospisil ~ 2006
*The Countess Of Flatbroke*, Mary Meriam ~ 2006
*Blue Glass Cities*, Mark Allinson ~ 2006
*Prolegomena To An Essay On Satire*, R. Nemo Hill ~2006
*William Montgomery*, Quincy R. Lehr ~ 2006

**ORDER ONLINE AT** exotbooks.com

www.ingramcontent.com/pod-product-compliance
Lightning Source LLC
Chambersburg PA
CBHW030914080526
44589CB00010B/307